THE FEMALE ENTREPRENEUR'S GUIDE TO

CREATING YOUR OWN WEBSITE

in a Weekend

RUTHANN BOWEN

ISBN 978-1-953449-27-6

CONTENTS

WELCOME FROM RUTHANN

I didn't start my career in web design. As a matter of fact, I didn't start my full-time web design agency until I was 50. Why do I tell you that? Because if I can do it, YOU can do it!

I know sometimes the technological side of things can get messy and confusing. I've had several conversations with female entrepreneurs bursting into tears because it was so overwhelming. But it doesn't have to be that way. That's why I've put together this easy-to-use guide that will catapult you past the overwhelm into confidently launching your beautiful website; one you are proud to show off and not run away in shame. The goal here is to keep it simple and give you the tools you need to actually get your website created—minus all the headaches and tears. It's as easy as carving out a few hours on the weekend, using this guide, and getting your website launched by Monday. You'll learn where to start and how to finish strong.

So, let's dive in and work our way to launching your pretty, powerful website!

"The quality of your website = the quality of your business."

RUTHANN BOWEN

DISCOVER YOUR AUDIENCE

"Your website is not about YOU.
It's about your ideal client."

RUTHANN BOWEN

Plato said, "Know thyself."

Marketers say, "Know your audience."

Knowing and understanding your target audience is the absolute first step when it comes to getting your website—and business—on the right path toward profit and success. Understanding who they are shapes the language and design of your website, allowing your business to truly speak to your customers. It defines and clarifies your message. It communicates in a way they understand and positions you as someone they can trust because you "get them."

One of the first things I tell my clients when we start the discovery process for their website is, *"Your website is not about YOU. It's about your ideal client."* This is a vital mindshift that needs to be made in the beginning of the process. Otherwise your website develops into a "hey, look at me!" and that's the kiss of death when it comes to connecting with your audience. It needs to reflect and resonate with THEM. So, the first thing we're going to do is spend some time figuring out your ideal client. It's the foundational step towards building a high converting website.

WHO IS *YOUR* TARGET AUDIENCE

The goal here is to understand your ideal customer intimately. You need to get in their heads. Put yourself in their shoes. What they think about. What they desire. When they read the messaging on your site they should be thinking to themselves, "It's like she's in my head!"

15 QUESTIONS TO HIT YOUR TARGET

Take a few minutes and write down your answers to the following questions and watch your ideal customer spring to life. You'll begin understanding them better. You'll become more familiar with their everyday life and how your service or product fits into their daily routine. And once you have that nailed down, you are on the right track to connecting and conversing with them in such a way that makes it irresistible for them to work with you.

YOUR IDEAL CLIENT PROFILE

1.   What's their name?

_____

2.   What's their age?

_____

3.   What's their marital status?

_____

4. Where do they live?

_____

5. What's their income?

_____

6. What's their occupation?

_____

7. What are their values?

_____

8. Where do they shop?

_____

9. Do they have kids?

_____

10. Do they go on vacation anywhere?

_____

11. Do they have a hobby?

_____

12. Do they read and if so what?

_____

13.   Where do they hang out?

_____

14.   Where do they shop?

_____

15.   What news do they watch?

_____

After spending some time writing out your answers, you'll start to recognize your ideal client. It will also help you realize who ISN'T your ideal client. Trust me. This will serve you well as you move forward in your business. There's nothing worse than working with someone who isn't the right fit for you. Also keep in mind, this exercise is an on-going process. As your business grows and you spend more time with your audience, you'll start to narrow down even more who the perfect client is for you.

Next, let's discover their pain points.

Now that you have a better idea who your ideal client is, next you need to figure out their pain points. Understanding the reasons why your target audience needs you is the key to ensuring your messaging and your website work successfully. Your business exists because you've come up with an idea that alleviates some sort of pain for them. It's the answer they are longing for and can't live without. But how do you ensure your website appeals to them in such a way that makes them choose to work with you and not your competitors?

Answering the following questions gets you closer to figuring out your message:

1. What are the three most common problems my target audience faces?

_____

_____

_____

_____

2. How does my target audience currently solve these problems?

_____

_____

_____

_____

3. How can my business help them solve it better? What do I offer that's different from my competitors?

_____

_____

_____

_____

Your answers will guide you to the best way of reaching and interacting with your ideal customer. They will help you determine what the best voice is to use (formal or more casual?), how best to communicate with them (long or short emails, direct messages on social media?), and what wording/messaging resonates with them. Getting into their heads gives you the roadmap needed to connect with them and ultimately build trust with them.

YOUR SOLUTION IS...

Now that you've figured out who your ideal client is and what their pain points are, it's time to list out your solutions. What answers do you provide that resonate with them? Revisit the top three issues your ideal client faces and write down your solutions:

Solution number one:

_____

_____

Solution number two:

_____

_____

Solution number three:

_____

_____

Using my own site, wixdesignher.com, as an example, I identified three pain points my ideal client deals with: they're busy, they're frustrated, they're non-techies.

PAIN POINT:	Busy
IDENTIFIER:	You've spent countless hours trying to figure out your website only to end up with more questions than answers.
SOLUTION:	We'll save you time.
WHAT TO DO:	Click the Call-to-Action button, "Yes! Please Help."

PAIN POINT:	Frustrated
IDENTIFIER:	You're banging your head on your desk because the 'easy' backend editor turned out to be more complicated than promised.
SOLUTION:	We'll eliminate your frustration.
WHAT TO DO:	Click the Call-to-Action button, "Yes, Please Help."

PAIN POINT:	Non-techie
IDENTIFIER:	You're tired of trying to figure it all out and are ready to hire a professional to finally get a website you love.
SOLUTION:	We've got this covered for you giving you the confidence you need moving forward with your online presence.
WHAT TO DO:	Click the Call-to-Action button, "Yes, Please Help."

Here are some ways you can continue to research and understand your target audience. As time goes on, you'll want to tweak and make changes to your messaging so you're always in touch with the pulse of what's going on with them.

Start A Conversation

Simply start talking with people. If you have a general idea who your customer is, start talking with them. Ask them the questions from above and uncover their pain points. Once you have a good idea of their pain points, you can then address more specifically how your solution to those nagging issues will benefit them.

Get Social

Listening in on social conversations will give you great insight to people's issues and pains. Join groups where your target market resides and pay close attention to the wording and phrasing they are using. Start a Word document and literally copy and paste these phrases. Then when it's time for you to write your copy for your website you can refer to this wording. Doing this not only shows your target audience you truly understand their pain but it also positions you as an expert to help them.

Check Out Your Competitors

More than likely, you aren't the only business in your market or industry. Visit your competitor's websites, get on their mailing lists, follow their social accounts—see what they are doing and how they are getting their message across. This helps you determine your own style and how best to communicate with your audience.

Survey says...

If striking up a conversation with someone isn't really your jam, ask questions in an online survey. You could even offer a coupon code for everyone who fills it out. You could put the survey on your website to drive traffic there. It's a win-win-win.

WHY SHOULD I WORK WITH YOU? (MAKE YOURSELF IRRESISTIBLE)

Identifying and understanding your target audience helps you create your unique content for your website. Shaping your language, images, tone, and mood throughout your website encourages your potential client or customer to engage with you. They see you understand them and can offer answers and value. Your research from this chapter has uncovered their pain points so don't be afraid to address them head on. Put your solution and answers right up front where it can't be missed. This draws in a deeper connection with your audience and moves them in the direction of working with you. (For a real, live example of this, visit wixdesignher.com and see how I address my target audience's pain points.)

✈ **ACTION STEP** *Complete the Ideal Client Profile section of this chapter.*

Once you've completed your Ideal Client Profile, you'll be ready to dive into the next section where we'll discover what content is and how you can make yours engaging and enticing. Let's get your visitors saying "Yes!" to your product or service.

DEFINE YOUR CONTENT

Content is King.

Somewhere along the line you probably heard the phrase, "Content is king." There's a reason for that. Because it is! Content is what helps drive traffic to your site. Content is what you are saying and how you are saying it. Content is what your audience is looking for from you. So, let's take a deeper look into your website content.

Your website content includes:
1. Professional photos
2. Engaging videos
3. Inspiring text

PROFESSIONAL PHOTOS

Humans are visual creatures. When we see an image it evokes an emotional response. That's why when it comes to making your online presence dynamic and engaging a huge part of that stems from high-quality, beautiful photography.

Images are a powerful tool to promote your business and quickly convey your message. They should grab your visitor's attention and keep it. Anyone landing on your site should immediately be able to tell what your business is about and what products or services you offer. The more professional and engaging your images the better chance you have of impressing your visitors and keeping them on your site longer.

WHERE TO START

First, ask yourself these questions:

1. What is the goal of my site?
2. What do I want my visitors to think and feel when they land on my site?

Your answers will guide you to the basic aesthetic concerning the images you choose. For example, are you running an online boutique with handmade jewelry where you need up-close, white background, sharp, product photos? Or maybe you run a childcare business that needs bright and cheerful colors?

A quick hop over to Pinterest and searching for your product or service is a great place to jumpstart your inspiration. Create your own mood board and see what you come up with. You can also search blogs and other websites of leaders (or even competitors) in your industry.

You can also find great inspiration offline. Magazines, art galleries, nature, books, a walk on a local trail...your options and sources are endless! The key is keeping an open mind and observing your surroundings. You never know when or where inspiration will strike.

TIP

There are some great FREE online sources for professional stock photos. Check these out:

Unsplash.com
Pexels.com
Pixabay.com

✒ **ACTION STEP** *Carve out a half hour to start searching for images and photos that reflect the mood, personality and feel of your business. Choose six that best represent your brand and reflect the mood and feel of your business. You will start to see themes emerging that you can use as a guide for your website design.*

PLAN YOUR PHOTOS

When thinking about your website, take a little time to plan what photos you are going to need. Here's a list of common areas photos are used on a website:

HERO IMAGE: The very first image people see when they land on your Home Page. Out of all the photos on your site, this one is a high priority. It needs to accurately reflect who you are and what you do. It doesn't necessarily have to be an exact image...but it does need to get across the mood and feel of what you do. Using the childcare business example from earlier, a picture of a smiling child playing with some toys would be an inspiring image to use.

ABOUT US/STAFF: Meeting the people "behind the scenes" is always fun so be sure to include a professional headshot of you and your team members. This gives credibility to your business as well as adds a personal touch. We like to work with people we know, so let your visitors know a little bit about you and the benefits of working with you.

PHYSICAL SPACE: Taking photos of your building or inside your office is another great way to let people take a peek inside your world. Plus, if people are making a trip to your physical store or building, it's always helpful to see what it looks like confirming you're in the right place.

PRODUCTS AND SERVICES: This is the nuts and bolts of your website. Include inspiring and eye-catching images promoting what you do or offer. For product photos, be sure to use a white background, proper lighting, and include multiple views or perspectives of the product if possible.

THE TRUTH ABOUT HIRING A PROFESSIONAL PHOTOGRAPHER

Making a small investment by hiring a professional photographer is the best thing you can do to boost your online presence. This one thing alone will elevate your site and show people that you care about what you're putting out there. Many times I've been asked,

"Can't I use my iphone? They take great pictures."

While camera technology has improved greatly, nothing takes the place of a professional photographer. They understand things like lighting, backgrounds, editing, resolution, and so much more. Remember, your website is a very visual medium so you want to make sure your images are high quality.

"But how can I afford a professional photographer? I'm just starting out and I have no money." (I know, I hear this quite often).

Here are a couple of ways:

1. Save.
   Nothing fancy.
   Simply, save.
   It should only cost a couple hundred dollars to get a professional headshot done. Use the power of a Google search and find local photographers in your area to get an idea of what they charge. Then simply start saving.

2. There are professional photographers who are just starting out that may have prices within your budget. Many times they are trying to build their portfolios and offer lower prices than a local photographer in greater demand. Do your research and keep digging. Ask around. Contact your local chamber of commerce. You might even find one you can barter with. There's a photographer out there just right for you and your budget. It's simply a matter of finding the right one.

✒ **ACTION STEP** *Whether it's for your headshot or product photos, research, find, and hire a professional photographer. It's an investment you won't regret.*

ENGAGING VIDEOS

Here are two compelling statistics according to Hubspot, an online marketing company, that should get you thinking about using video content on your website:

1. "Including video on a landing page can increase conversion rates 80%."
2. "After watching a video, 64% of users are more likely to buy a product online."

OK. If that's not enough reason to include video on your site I don't know what is.

10 REASONS AND WAYS TO INCORPORATE VIDEO ON YOUR WEBSITE:

1. Enhance your website user-experience
2. Demonstrate a product, service, or activity
3. Share your expertise
4. Drive traffic to your website
5. Earn money
6. Promote a sale or special event
7. Give your business a personal face
8. Engage customers with your brand
9. Encourage regular visits to your site
10. Stand out from your competition

Fortunately, the good news is you don't have to hire a big, expensive video production company in order to grab attention. Think with Google conducted in-depth research with Omnicom Media Group surveying 3,000 people, ages 13-64 to find out what they determined to be "high quality content" when it came to YouTube ads. The findings were surprising. The three things that emerged from this study were:

1. Beautiful storytelling trumps video production value
2. Niches can be huge
3. Premium is personal

Need some video ideas to get you started? Here are a few:

1. How-to regarding a product you sell
2. Introduce yourself and put it on your About page
3. Have a special offer? Explain more about it in a video.
4. Behind the scenes at your store/office
5. Interview employees
6. Feature customer testimonials (get their permission, first)

⤳ **ACTION STEP** *Create a 30 second video introducing yourself and put it on your home page or about page.*

Here's a short sample script you could use on your About page to get you started:

"Hi, I'm _____ and if you've landed here then you might be experiencing (list out one or two pain points your audience experiences). I've been there and I know how frustrating that can be. But I've also learned how to move out of that frustration to a place of success. If you're ready to break free and move forward towards (list one or two of your solutions), I can help you do that. You can sign up for my free monthly newsletter with specific tips or you can sign up for one of my packages where you get customized, private instruction from me. Either way, you'll be on your way on the fast track to success. Looking forward to connecting with you!"

INSPIRING TEXT

Web design is hard enough. Coming up with compelling copy to turn visitors into customers? That seems downright daunting! But never fear. With a few simple guidelines you can start writing converting copy in no time.

Focus, Focus, Focus

I tell my clients every website is like a fingerprint. It's completely unique. (At least it should be...never, never, never copy someone else's website).

Your business is YOUR business. Everything on your website reflects you and your business. So write content that communicates your unique message clearly and concisely. One of the biggest mistakes I come across on websites is too much information. You don't need to be wordy. As a matter of fact, if someone sees too much wording on a site they may immediately bounce because they don't have the time to sift through to get to what they're looking for. Your visitor is going to scan anyway. Rarely does anyone read every word on a website these days.

Stay focused on addressing your visitor's pain points with your solutions.

Say it fast

Can you describe your business in 30 seconds or less? The classic elevator pitch helps you define and describe your business in about 2-4 sentences. It focuses on the most important points of your business and what you provide. It's a succinct and persuasive sales pitch. So make it memorable. Going through this process will help you weed out the unnecessary and get to the golden nuggets of your content.

Here's one of the 30 second commercials I use when networking:

> Hi, I'm Ruthann Bowen, founder of Wix DesignHer where I help female entrepreneurs get a pretty, powerful website. Most women starting out in their business are DIYing everything, including their website. They quickly get frustrated with the technology, find they don't have the time to 'get it right' and end up thinking maybe they should just quit. I help these women stay on the path to success by offering affordable web designs and website coaching so they can get a high converting website that kickstarts their business.

✈ **ACTION STEP** *Write out your 30-second commercial.*

KEEP IT SIMPLE

Your readers will get a sense of who you are through your content. Avoid complicated jargon and technical terms so your visitors feel welcome and understood. They need to know there's an actual human being behind the business. If it works with your brand, throw in some wit and fun and use a conversational tone. Remember, though, if it doesn't feel natural to you, it won't read naturally to them.

Here are a few examples of web design industry jargon that probably doesn't mean much to the average female entrepreneur just starting her business:

AJAX (Asynchronous JavaScript and XML)
Above the fold
Below the fold
Cache
DNS
Favicon
Hero Image
Wireframe
Front End
Back End
CMS (Content Management System)

See what I mean? If I had used those words in my copy you probably would've bounced off that page immediately with more questions than answers. As my former mentor used to say to me, "Ruthann, explain it to me like I'm a two year old." What he was training me to do was putting complex ideas and thoughts into simple terms. You need to do this as well, because wording and terminology that you know and use on a daily basis may be completely foreign to your visitor.

ACTION STEP *Identify your industry jargon to steer away from using.*

When it comes to writing for your website sometimes the most obvious information gets overlooked. NAP refers to Name, Address, Phone. These are the most important pieces of information people look for when landing on a site.

Name
Believe it or not, I was recently visiting a business coaching website and her name was nowhere to be found. Not in the header, not in the copy, not in the contact form. Zip. Nada. No name. Whether you are a personal brand or have a company name, please be sure to include it on your website!

Address
The reason you want to have some type of location is because this helps get you found in local Google searches. However, many female entrepreneurs are freelancers so putting your home address out there isn't smart. The last thing you want is some random, strange person arriving on your doorstep. A few ways to get around this is by simply using your town name or closest city. Or, get a PO Box. You can also list out the counties you service which also helps in the local searches.

Phone
If you use your personal cell phone for calls I highly suggest not to put that on your website. Google offers free numbers you can use that will ring directly to your phone. It's a much safer way to put your business out there without compromising your personal information. Check out voice.google.com to find out more and get your own free business phone number.

USE POWER WORDS AND PHRASES

Some words have more punch than others. In order to achieve convert-ing copy, include power words and phrases throughout your website. Don't just insert a word in a sentence because it's a power word, though. Make sure it reads naturally and adds to the flow of your sentence or paragraph.

Here are 31 power words to jumpstart your converting copy:

Become an insider	Piece of cake
Behind the scenes	Power(ful)
Best	Prize
Big	Remarkable
Dazzling	Riveting
Effective	Save
Eye-opening	Simple
Giveaway	Straightforward
Instantly	Six-figure
Interesting	Skyrocket
Invitation Only	Soar
Kickstart	Unconventional
Manifest	Unlock
Mindblowing	Up-sell
No nonsense	Value
No sweat	

✒ **ACTION STEP** *Come up with one paragraph or a Call-To-Action using power words.*

_____

_____

_____

_____

_____

_____

_____

_____

_____

_____

_____

_____

_____

HIERARCHY

Hierarchy keeps your site organized. It allows your readers to stay focused on a specific path. Organizing your site with the following basic hierarchy ensures your most important information gets seen...and ideally, engages them to click through.

- **SHORT HEADLINE:** A simple sentence describing what the page is all about.

- **SUBHEADER:** Slightly longer sentence encouraging the visitor to read more.

- **BODY TEXT:** Most pages call for some more in-depth content. On your About page, this would be the story of your business. On a product page, this might be a gallery of products with product descriptions. This is where you'd also include customer testimonials, reviews and more.

- **CALL TO ACTION:** Include a valuable offer for your readers with an action to take, whether it's making a purchase, joining a mailing list, or getting in touch.

Phew! That's a lot to think about! But you made it through and are prepared with what you need to create a high converting website using just the right messaging for your business. Now that you have all of your content figured out it's time to move forward with the design of your website.

DESIGN YOUR WEBSITE:
A Page-By-Page Guide

"38% of people will stop engaging with a website if the content/layout is unattractive."

ADOBE

Wow!

That's the response you're going for when designing your website.

Just as when a bride walks down the aisle evoking that "Ahhhh" response from her guests, THAT's the emotion you want from your visitors when they land on your website. You want them to go "Wow!" the moment they land on the first page. It should look beautiful with no detail overlooked. It should fit you...aka, your business...perfectly. It needs to represent who you are and what you do with elegance and perfection. No matter what industry you work in, your website shouldn't look like you just threw it together. This is the biggest marketing piece of your business so don't skimp when it comes to your online look and presence.

Side Note: As you start and build your business, keep in mind the philosophy of investing in this necessary expense. Hiring a professional web designer could be one of the smartest moves you make as you launch your online presence. One of the biggest pain points for my target audience is the frustration that comes with creating their own website.

Can you DIY it? Yes, absolutely. *Should* you? Only you can answer that honestly. Sometimes the hassle, headache, and headbanging wastes precious time you could spend on other areas of growing your business.

TIP

"Curious how your website could look designed by a pro? Check out the affordable options for design as well as website coaching at wixdesignher.com"

The goal here is for "Love at first site."

Getting your visitors to instantly fall head-over-heels with your business through your website takes a little bit of design savvy. Here are a few pro tips to keep in mind:

1. Stay current with design trends. Just as fashions fade in and out, so do website designs.
2. Ensure your most important info stands out, i.e. CTAs (Calls-to Action, titles, etc.) Your user is only going to spend a couple of seconds eyeing up whether or not they want to stay on your site so make it as easy as possible for them to find that all important info.
3. Don't play all your cards at once. Too much information right away overloads your visitor and they give up. Manage the amount of info you are giving them up front and use a lot of white space.

PAGES

Whether you have 5 or 500 pages, there are some must-haves to include on your site.

Home Page

With only 3 seconds to grab your visitor's attention, your Home Page lives under a lot of pressure to perform. Consider this page the welcome mat to your business. Typically it's the first place people land so you want to be sure it clearly defines your business. Using the three tips mentioned above—stay current with design trends, make your most important information stand out, and don't overload with too much information—will ensure you get the winning combination.

There are several questions your Home Page needs to answer for your visitors quickly:

- Does this business understand my pain points?
- Do they provide the solution I need?
- What am I supposed to do?

Remember the pain points you identified earlier for your target audience? This is the page to identify those issues clearly and concisely. Here's an example of the pain points an ideal client for a nutrition coach might address on the Home Page:

PAIN POINT: Busy

IDENTIFIER: You're working full time, you have family responsibilities for kids and parents, and you're running around all day with little time to yourself no less having to come up with nutritious meals.

SOLUTION: We'll save you time.

WHAT TO DO: Click the Call-to-Action button, "Get your weekly menu here."

PAIN POINT:	No motivation
IDENTIFIER:	You know deep inside you should exercise and eat better but you aren't motivated to take that next step.
SOLUTION:	We'll provide the motivation you need.
WHAT TO DO:	Click the Call-to-Action button, "Start Now!"

PAIN POINT:	Little knowledge of where to start
IDENTIFIER:	You're unsure about what foods are the best for you and your family with all the different diets out there. Which one is right for you?
SOLUTION:	We totally get it and have a simple three step questionnaire to figure out the easiest path to success for you and your family.
WHAT TO DO:	Click the Call-to-Action button, "Get started today."

Here's a basic Home Page Template to get you started:

My headline is:

_____

My subheader is:

_____

My body copy is:

_____

_____

_____

_____

_____

_____

_____

_____

_____

_____

My Call-to-Action is:

_____

_____

Check out this Home Page example for inspiration.
thebowenagency.wixsite.com/homepagesample

About Page

While the About page may seem lower in priority, it's actually a great place to:

1. Tell your story
2. Share your value
3. Provide your solution
4. Include a CTA

Everyone has a story. The decision to start your own business most likely was a journey so tell your visitors about the process. Share why you're doing this and what prompted you to take the leap and start your own business.

Be yourself. People find it easier to trust human beings so don't feel like you need to write "stiff, corporate, professional" copy. Use your own voice and remember to avoid industry jargon that won't resonate with your readers. Straight-talk keeps confusion away. You don't want people wondering what you do so tell them clearly and effectively.

Make sure your grammar is correct and everything is spelled right. But always make sure you sound friendly and real.

People work with people they like. Your About Page gives you the space to show off your personality. In just a couple of paragraphs show who you are and what you do as well as your products or services. Are you a little quirky? Great! Paint that picture for your visitors here. Are you very casual and laid back? Incorporate that feel in your copy.

Use photos. This, of course, is a great page to use that professional headshot we talked about earlier. It's also a great place to showcase the inside of your office, building, shop, desk, wherever it is you work. Behind the scenes gives your readers a glimpse into the day-to-day operations of your business and humanizes it helping them connect to what you do.

✒ ACTION STEP *Write your story. Here are some prompts to get you thinking:*

> *Why did you start this business?*
> *Where do you want this business to be in five years?*
> *What do you like most about your business?*
> *What makes your business different?*

_____

_____

_____

_____

_____

_____

_____

_____

_____

_____

_____

_____

Services/Product Page

It doesn't matter if you are a jewelry maker, yoga teacher, or business coach, your service and product pages are the bread and butter of your website. Be sure to showcase all the goodness you offer in a way that compels people to buy from or work with you.

Don't forget to include these things on your professional services pages or product pages:

- A brief overview of your products/services
- Catchy but clear product descriptions
- Prominent, easy-to-find call-to-actions
- Professional product images (no cell phone pics, please!)
- Customer reviews and/or testimonials

✐ **ACTION STEP** *List your services with a brief description of each or one product description. (Use power words if possible and appropriate)*

_____

_____

_____

_____

_____

_____

Contact Page

A stunning Contact Page includes making it as easy as possible for people to get in touch with you. Include the NAP must-haves: Name, Address, Phone. Also feature your email address and social links so people can follow you. And adding a friendly welcome sentence encouraging your visitors to get in touch with you wouldn't hurt, either.

Don't forget...if any of this information changes, update your contact info immediately.

If your business has a physical location with a brick and mortar building, add a map so customers can easily identify where you're located. List your opening hours so visitors know when they can drop by.

✒ **ACTION STEP** *Write out your NAP and list your hours, if applicable.*

Every Page

Having the following elements on every page ensures people have what they need at their fingertips:

1. Your logo/business name: This can be in the left hand corner, middle, or right hand corner in your header. Just be sure it's in the same place on every page. A good web design practice is to link your Home Page to your logo. This makes for easy navigation.

2. Your primary CTA (call-to-action): This is the action you want your visitors to take when they are on your site. Make it highly visible so it can't be missed.
3. Social Icons: Add social icons to your site so people can easily follow you on your social channels. It's a great way to stay engaged with your customers.
4. Contact details: Not just for a contact page...include the basics in your footer (or header, wherever it makes the most sense for your business) including Name, Phone Number, Address and Email.

DESIGN

Taking on the challenge of DIYing your own website can be overwhelming at times. Fortunately, you don't have to start from scratch as there are plenty of templates you can use as a springboard for your site. Check out Wix.com where you'll find hundreds of free templates to use in all sorts of industries. Just pick one you like and customize with your own information.

When people ask me to review their website for professional feedback, there are two common issues I come across frequently: over usage of fonts and poor color choices.

While web design has more to it than fonts and colors, I'm going to focus on these two since they seem to cause the most confusion.

Fonts
First of all, what is a font?

Font = The collection of characters that describe a typeface. Fonts vary according to size, weight (thickness), and style.

Example:
    Typeface = **Helvetica**
    Font = Helvetica Neue
    Font = Helvetica Neue Light

Serif or Sans Serif

The next step to understanding typefaces is the difference between a Serif and Sans Serif typeface.

Serifs are the slight projections finishing off a stroke of a letter such as this:

Serif fonts have a classical, elegant, and traditional feel.

Sans Serif are the typefaces that don't have the slight projections off the letter strokes such as this:

Serif fonts have a modern, clean, universal feel.

When deciding on which fonts to use for your business keep in mind that most importantly it needs to be readable across all the different platforms (smartphones, tablets, desktops, laptops, etc). Make sure what you pick compliments your website design reflecting the mood and personality of your business. If it checks off all those boxes, you've found your font!

Font Pairing

There are a LOT of fonts to choose from when it comes to deciding which ones are right for you. The temptation to use all the ones you like is very real. **However, stick to using only 2-3 on your site because**

when you start using more than that it creates a chaotic feel. And you don't want that.

Choosing which fonts work best together can get confusing. There are so many great choices out there it's hard to narrow it down. Trust me, I get it!

Fortunately, there are many great resources you can turn to in order to get inspiration and guidance. This one is my favorite:

Canva: Ultimate Guide to Font Pairing
www.canva.com/learn/the-ultimate-guide-to-font-pairing/

Font Size
Keep in mind, the main goal here is readability. Before you get started, though, assign one size to each type of text. For example:

Header: **Helvetica Neue Bold**
Subheading: *Helvetica Neue Italic*
Body: Helvetica Neue

Heading/Title
Right now titles seem to be trending toward bigger is better. 36 pixels (px) is the average title font size but make sure whatever size you use balances with your body copy as well.

Subtitle
Your subtitle size should be a size in between your body copy and heading. Again, keep balance in mind.

Body Copy
When keeping readability in mind, 16px is optimum. The popular choice is 12–14px but this can sometimes be too small for optimal viewing and accessibility.

Where to find the best fonts?

There are many places to go to find just the right font for your business. You can find free fonts or pay for one. It's really just a matter of what you feel is right for you and your budget.

Free Fonts:
Google Fonts: *fonts.google.com/*
Font Squirrel: *www.fontsquirrel.com/*
Font Space: *www.fontspace.com/*
Fontasy: *www.fontasy.de/?lang=en*

If you can't find anything for free, consider going to these sites where you can purchase a font.

Paid Fonts:
Font Shop: *www.fontshop.com/*
Fonts.com: *www.fonts.com/*
Creative Market: *creativemarket.com/fonts*

Whether you decide to use a free or paid font, these resources will guide you to the perfect font for your business.
(For more info on picking the right font check out the blog post over at *wixdesignher.com* on "The Importance of Choosing the Right Font")

✒ **ACTION STEP** *Research fonts and write the names of some you like. Pick 2-3 from your list for your website.*

Fonts I like for my website:

_____

_____

_____

_____

_____

Color Scheme

Colors play a powerful part in our everyday lives. They evoke emotions and influence behavior. They influence a feeling or mood. And you can use that power to your advantage when designing your website.

Did you know that, according to Buffer, 90% of our assessment on a product is based on color alone? The same goes for your choice of website colors. If you don't like a site's colors, chances are you won't stay on it for very long.

Playing With Color

You probably remember from grade school learning about primary (red, blue and yellow), secondary (orange, green, violet), and tertiary colors (a mix of both primary and secondary colors). When thinking about these colors keep in mind certain color combinations create harmony and balance while others create chaos. Remember, when it comes to your website we're striving for balance. So choose colors that are easy on the eye and make people want to stay.

Color Inspiration

Not sure where to start when it comes to picking out the right colors for your website? Check out these resources that will jumpstart your imagination:

DesignSeeds: *www.design-seeds.com/*
Canva: *www.canva.com/*
Coolors: *coolors.co*

For a complete listing of colors and what moods/emotions they instill, head over to this blog post: "How Your Website Colors Can Increase Sales" *www.eastcampcreative.com/post/how-your-website-colors-can-increase-sales*

✍ **ACTION STEP** *Head over to Canva and put together a mood board featuring five colors you like along with the 2-3 fonts you picked. You can add the images from the previous action step under content and voila! You have a brand board that will keep you focused as you design your site.*

You are so close to launch! Once you have your website design finalized and ready, there's one last thing to check off the list. Read on...

DOMINATE YOUR SEO
My Site Is Done! Now What?

You can have the most beautiful website in the world, but if no one can find you online then your business won't grow.

SEO, Search Engine Optimization, is the key to getting found online. It's a very big subject that I'll briefly discuss here to get you started.

UNDERSTANDING THE BASICS OF SEO

The journey your customer takes online begins with a search engine such as Google, Bing, Yahoo, and others like them. Google, of course, is the largest and most powerful, so when the discussion of Search Engine Optimization comes up, most of the time business owners mean getting found on Google.

Everyone wants to be on page one of Google's SERP, Search Engine Results Page. It's a coveted spot and depending on your business, keywords, and niche, it can be difficult to achieve. But here are six things you can do to help organically rank higher in search engine results.

Submit your site to Google.
Google uses bots that continuously crawl content on the web, so at some point your website will get found. To speed up the process, you can submit your site directly to Google announcing to the world your presence. Simply head over to Google Search Console, a web service by Google,

provided free of charge for webmasters, which allows them to check indexing status and optimize visibility of their websites. Basically, it's a good way of alerting Google that your business website exists and giving it that little push to speed up the indexing process.

Find out how to submit your site to Google here;
www.google.com/webmasters/tools/submit-url

Leave A Link Trail

Another great way to get your site noticed is to direct those bots with links in other places throughout the web. When the bots "read" those blue text hyperlinks it's sending them directly to your website. This is why getting a shout out from someone who has a big blog following is helpful in getting noticed by the search engines. But even if you don't have big influencer friends, you can send those bots to your website via your social media profiles and online directories such as Yelp. Not only is it super convenient for people to click on these links, but each location you place that link provides a superhighway directly to your beautiful website.

Using Keywords

When your prospective client opens their phone or computer and starts searching for your business, what are they typing in to find you? Those words and phrases are called "keywords." Once someone types in those keywords, the search engine starts looking for the websites that best match those keywords. And those are the websites that end up on the search engine results page. This is why you want to make sure you're using those keywords throughout your site's content and SEO settings.

There are keyword tools you can use to do a little more in-depth keyword research for your business. They can help you find out what the most commonly used words and phrases are for your business and industry. Using these words throughout your content and SEO settings lets Google know your site is a good match for that query.

Check out this blog post with free keyword tools you can use: *www.wixdesignher.com/post/free-keyword-research-help-for-the-beginner*

Meta Tag Magic

So just how do you get Google to recognize your site? Meta tags. Meta tags are the elements that make up a web page's listing. The blue letters you see on a search engine results page is the SEO title and the black/gray description underneath is the meta description. It's not text directly used on your website, but choosing clear, concise wording for these sections is imperative for getting your visitor to click on your link. This is also the place to use your keywords. It's high-value real estate when it comes to your business because this could very well be the first place people find out about you. So be sure you make it click-worthy.

Optimize for mobile

There's nothing worse than searching for something on your smartphone, finding a business website that seems to be the perfect match, only to land on it and have to do the "two-finger-swipe" to zoom in. Or to find the content and images are cut off from the display screen. Ugh! Since Google wants to keep their browsers happy, as of July 1, 2019, it is now ranking all new websites via their mobile version first. So be sure your website is mobile friendly. This means all information and images fit correctly on the mobile screen.

Be Local with Google My Business

Local SEO helps browsers find matches for what they are looking for locally. This is great for business owners who have a brick and mortar store they want people to find. In order to boost your local business presence in search engine results be sure to fill out the Google My Business. This directory of local business listings populates what appears on Google Maps. Additionally, it also displays what's in the "local pack," the map and three business options that show up in a box at the top of a search query. It doesn't take long to fill out the Google My Business information but Google will send you a verification code in order to finish the process. They typically send the verification code via a postcard which can take up to five days to receive. Taking this step is just one more way of alerting Google that your business is a good match to suggest to its users when they use your keywords.

Set up your Google My Business account here:
www.google.com/business

RE-CAP

I know this is a lot to take in and you might be feeling a little over-whelmed. Or excited! As an entrepreneur there are always a mixture of feelings you might be experiencing at any one time. That's totally normal!

Now, let's recap. Here is a simple checklist of the elements you need to take you from "OMG What is a website?" to "love at first site." Following these steps will have your new website up in no time.

ULTIMATE DIY WEBSITE CHECKLIST

- ☐ Get your domain name for your business website if you don't already have one. You can get one at Wix, GoDaddy, or BlueHost.

- ☐ Complete the Ideal Client Profile on page 10 to understand who you are reaching.

- ☐ Choose the platform you're going to use to build your site. I recommend Wix because of its very user friendly interface but there are other options such as Squarespace and Weebly as well.**

- ☐ Grab your free Google Voice number if you need one (voice.google.com)

- ☐ Research and hire a professional photographer for your headshots and/or product images.

- ☐ Set up your social media accounts if you don't have them for your business yet.

- ☐ Create a logo if you don't have one yet.

- ☐ Choose a template from your website builder or if you're very adventurous, start from scratch!

- ☐ Research photos and images that best represent your business or brand

- ☐ Research and choose three fonts to use on your site.

- ☐ Research and choose the colors you'll be using on your site.

- ☐ Research your keywords and use them on your site's page titles, descriptions, and throughout your copy.

- ☐ Create your site.

- ☐ Proof your site/test all links.

- ☐ Launch your site!

SHARE YOUR CREATION

Congratulations! You made it!

You are now equipped with the foundational basics to deliver a pretty and powerful website. Remember, this is just the beginning. Getting your website up is the first step. After that it takes proper care and maintaining to ensure it's the high converting machine you want it to be.

Starting a business and living the life of an entrepreneur is not for the faint of heart. It takes grit, resilience, and a whole lot of hustle. Getting found online is one of the biggest keys to your success. And with this guide you have the map you need to ensure you grow your business with an impressive online presence.

I'd love to see what you come up with! Please share your website with me as I'd love to celebrate this very big step in your business journey. Feel free to email your link to the email address below.

Here's to your greatest success for your business and your life! You've got this!

Stay creative,

Ruthann Bowen

Let's stay in touch:
ruthann@thebowenagency.com
Facebook: *www.facebook.com/groups/wixdesignher*
LinkedIn: *www.linkedin.com/in/ruthann-bowen-0b9382107*
YouTube: *www.youtube.com/channel/UCnKxww7Qef1spfrL6U8bTzQ*
Instagram: *www.instagram.com/wixdesignher*

ABOUT RUTHANN

Ruthann Bowen, co-owner and chief marketing officer for Eastcamp Creative, is an inspiring and business-minded web designer located in the greater Pittsburgh area. Her passion is working with female entrepreneurs so she started Wix DesignHer helping them build pretty, powerful websites. As a Wix Expert, she teaches business-related classes showing people how to design using the easy drag-and-drop website building platform. Exercising the experience gained from her background in PR, she also holds workshops focused on the power of utilizing branding, social media and search engine optimization for small businesses. Ruthann has been a guest presenter at Belmont University, Grove City College, and Butler County Community College on the topics of blogging and content creation. She has also contributed to Business News Daily and Best Company on the importance of professional web design. Find out more about Ruthann Bowen at wixdesignher.com.

**There are plenty of platforms available for building your website. I personally have built on WordPress, Squarespace and Wix. Based on my experience, I find Wix to be the best platform for creativity, function, and ease of use for entrepreneurs just starting out. I encourage you to do your own research to find out which one will best suit your needs. But in case you're wondering, below is a list of the Top Ten reasons why I choose Wix:

Wix offers many features to build your own professional website. My Top Ten for using Wix include:

1. Industry leading SEO. You can run your site through the Wix SEO Wiz which is your own personalized SEO plan using your keywords and offers the ability of submitting your site directly to Google.

2. Easy drag-n-drop editor for flexible design. Want to move an image over? Don't like where your text sits? No problem. Just click on it and drag it to where you want it. Honestly, it doesn't get more simple than this.

3. Wix Media Library. Want to choose from literally thousands of free images you can filter and sort to your liking? Wix has its own media library as well access to Unsplash right in the editor. Convenient and fast.

4. Logo Maker. Need a logo for your business? Check out the logo maker available right in your dashboard.

5. Robust CRM included. Look no further than your Wix dashboard to find a workflow where leads from your site are captured. Set up your own customized process to track and connect with those leads turning them into paying customers. Easily set up auto email responses to respond immediately so a lead is never lost.

6. Wix apps. Quickly add a blog, music, video, events, bookings, ecommerce, forum, FAQs, and so much more making your site the go-to for your customers.

7. Accept payments, send out quotes and invoices, keep track of subscriptions and payment plans. All conveniently located within a click or two in your dashboard.

8. Analytics. Wix has its own analytics for your site including visits, bookings and purchases. Pick the time frame you want from the last seven days to the last 90 days. No Google analytics needed for just a quick synopsis of how your traffic is doing.

9. Wix app. Get notifications every time someone is on your site. Start a conversation with them answering their questions and moving them toward the sale with the easy-to-use chat feature.

10. Post directly to social media. Get customizable Facebook and Instagram posts right in your dashboard. No need to hop over to another platform to make your stunning social posts. Keep in touch right from your Wix account.

RESOURCES

Hop on over to wixdesignher.com and find resources, freebies, helpful articles, and so much more!

Here's a handy list of the resources mentioned throughout this book:

PAGE 39   Home Page example:
           https://thebowenagency.wixsite.com/homepagesample

PAGE 47   Canva: Ultimate Guide to Font Pairing:
           https://www.canva.com/learn/the-ultimate-guide-to-font-pairing/

PAGE 48   Google Fonts: *https://fonts.google.com/*

PAGE 48   Font Squirrel: *https://www.fontsquirrel.com/*

PAGE 48   Font Space: *https://www.fontspace.com/*

PAGE 48   Fontasy: *http://www.fontasy.de/?lang=en*

PAGE 48   Font Shop: *https://www.fontshop.com/*

PAGE 48   Fonts.com: *https://www.fonts.com/*

PAGE 48   Creative Market: *https://creativemarket.com/fonts*

PAGE 50   Design Seeds: *https://www.design-seeds.com/*

Page 50   Canva: *https://www.canva.com/*

PAGE 50   Coolors: *https://coolors.co/*

RUTHANN'S SOCIAL LINKS

Facebook *https://www.facebook.com/groups/wixdesignher*

LinkedIn *https://www.linkedin.com/in/ruthann-bowen-0b9382107/*

YouTube *https://www.youtube.com/channel/UCnKxww7Qef1spfrL6U8bTzQ*

Instagram *https://www.instagram.com/wixdesignher/*